# The House of Marriage

# The House of Marriage

POEMS

Erin Hanusa

LOUISIANA STATE UNIVERSITY PRESS

BATON ROUGE

This publication is supported in part by an award from the National Endowment for the Arts.

Published by Louisiana State University Press

An LSU Press Paperback Original

Manufactured in the United States of America
First printing

Designer: Laura Roubique Gleason
Typeface: Deepdene display with Minion Pro text
Printer and binder: Thomson-Shore, Inc.

Library of Congress Cataloging-in-Publication Data

Hanusa, Erin.
The house of marriage : poems / Erin Hanusa.
p. cm.
"An LSU Press paperback original"—T.p. verso.
ISBN 978-0-8071-3299-9 (pbk. : alk. paper)
I. Title.
PS3608.A7237H68 2008
811'.6—dc22

2007015681

The author would like to thank the editors of the following magazines, in which the poems listed first appeared (some in slightly different form or under different titles): *iris,* "The White Desert" (2003); *Quarterly West,* "A Prayer for Beginning," as "Prime: A Prayer for Beginning" (1998/99); *Southern Review,* "Double Birth," "Hard Days," and "The House of Marriage" (all 2005); *Sow's Ear Review,* "For an Unnamed Brother" (2003). She would also like to thank the University of Virginia for a Poe-Faulkner Fellowship.

Much love and many thanks to the following incomparable people: Erika Baxter, Jeff Berger-White, Danielle Chapman, Kelly Cherry, Burke Davis, Rita Dove, John Easterly, Mary Esselman, Marie Kaczorek, Catherine L. Kadair, Jesse Lee Kercheval, Jon Loomis, Whitney Morrill, Laura Norby, Greg Orr, Lisa Russ Spaar, Ellie Stanford, Ron Wallace, Charles Wright, and Cero Zuccarello.

Deepest gratitude to my father and sister. To all my family: thank you, thank you, thank you.

The paper in this book meets the guidelines for permanence and durability of the Committee on Production Guidelines for Book Longevity of the Council on Library Resources. ♾

*for Kelly and Burke,*
*good shepherds*

*and, always,*
*for Cero*

# Contents

i A PRAYER FOR BEGINNING

A Prayer for Beginning 3

In Baxter, Tennessee 5

The White Desert 6

Breast Self-Exam 7

Early Kitten 9

To M, on Memory 10

What the Angel Gabriel Said 11

Hard Days 12

ii HOW WE LEARNED TO LET GO

Lord's Prayer 15

Double Birth 16

Notes on Summer 17

How We Learned to Let Go 19

Her Hair 20

A Family of Expatriates from the Territories of Crazy 21

Late Arrival 22

October 23

Beachgrass 24

A Bridge-Building Competition 25

Duty 26

Elegy for My Father's Third Family 29

Place of Last Escape 30

Interlude 31

My Father's Fruit Trees 32

Acquittal 33

The Tourist 34

## iii LETTERS FROM THE ELISION


Letters from the Elision 37

The Chapter of Faults 38

*Dearest S* 41

*My S—* 42

Anthem 43

*My dear S* 45

Letter Home 46

*My drifting S* 47

*Dear S* 48

*My ache, my S—* 49


## iv THE HOUSE OF MARRIAGE


The Difficulty of Compline on a Train 53

For an Unnamed Brother 54

The House of Marriage 55

Conception 56

# i A PRAYER FOR BEGINNING

## A Prayer for Beginning

When we are born, we cry that we are come
To this great stage of fools.

—Shakespeare, *King Lear*

The faint sonogram is like
an FBI reconnaissance photo,
the body's curves and rushes chalked in, the glint
of an add-a-pearl spine just begun.

You are black and white,
trapped in two dimensions,
but I imagine you as the star of a photo essay,
awash in a murmur of furry light, bright
as sun seen through a closed eyelid.

Out here, our only pearls are flecks
of light in the sleepy clouds, the numb gray
all we could summon on the day
of your parents' marriage.

Each of them was once like you,
with skin pale and luminous
like the inside of an oyster shell,
as exact and complete there,
as perfect. We seem to lose

the things we know, we forget
ourselves and become
this human fugue of waste:
the haphazard begetting,
woman with her ceaseless needs,
man with his lycanthropy.

You will be born knowing
more than we did.
Already terra cotta, deep red plush, viscous white

must color the orderly room
of your preparation. Though you show us only
your back, hands clasped secretively
in front of you, we are unsurprised:

who can fault your reluctance to share
the steadiness of precision multiplication,
the same geometry that unfurls needles
on pines, yellow petals on African daisies,
the tones of the golden rectangle.

# In Baxter, Tennessee

A T-intersection; we've come
to some wrong. He goes in
to ask directions and
I cross the road. Weeds

twine my ankles
like begging cats. Thick
water fills the low ditch;
then, ten dropped suns

caught on the tines
of a hayrake. There's no sign
of use on it, discs bright
as Elvis's hall of records.

Its stillness puzzles me;
all this burnished grass
bordered by black fences,
and its fingers are flexed

but empty. What purpose,
this beauty?

## The White Desert

In the stillness of the windbreak
we sleep, each night colder than the one before.
As we awaken Mansour bakes

the tire-sized round of bread in the sand,
piles it with hot stones, slaps grit off
with the flat of his hand. The indolent

ocean of the desert furls
out from our fire, the huddled island
of dust-tongued travelers drinking tea.

*This is a picture of my mother,* says Mansour,
*you look like her.* Shining black wings of hair
folded gently about a round white face.

After breakfast we pack the truck
for another country town whose children
don't cry for *baksheesh* but run alongside

as we drive. Between the houses
laundry lines dangle paper temples
for Ramadan. At sunset,

Mansour builds the fire so the Muslim men
can eat their dinner quickly and get to work
on the campers' evening meal.

Mansour shells lima beans while he eats. The fed men
sing songs, roast a chicken on hot coals.
My fingers twist in the swell of silky pods.

Men are dancing. The hungry campers wait
on their sleeping bags, watch stars
bloom out of the January sky.

## Breast Self-Exam

The directions dangle from
the shower curtain rod.
*Raise arm above head—*
you are a swan, beautiful,
white or black with water shedding
off like tears.
The basic technique
is to work in a pattern—
unhaphazard, gridlike or spiral,
some motion that is regular and slow.
*Press, don't stroke—*
this is the detective at your breast,
not the dark-limbed lover.
These are a stranger's fingers
at their occupation, as fussy for smoothness
as the princess atop her thousand mattresses.

In the shower you think of push-up bras,
and the study you read about the way
they condense flesh, shoving it
into cruel shapes that breed tumors.
That black one your friend passed on to you
hangs on its hook in the closet like a loaded weapon.
You wear it in times of emergency,
a magnet that draws in touch.

All men are breast men, it seems,
but not in the cheapened way
movies and magazines would have you believe.
Besides the locker room girls,
no one ever said yours were too small—
just soft, white, tipped raspberry, and enough
to fit into the palms of his hands.

The two tiny radiation targets
buzzed like fruit flies

on the scan of your grandmother's breast.
You remember them

now, while searching your own
unblemished flesh, your life's companion
for those dark dots
that may flicker inside.
The slick skin moves in waves
beneath your businesslike fingers,
the only fingers your body knows,
the only reason you allow
to touch yourself.

## Early Kitten

Its face, a sketch—
twin eye-flaps

on a sucked red gumdrop,
nostril-specks, etched

curve of lip,
a dent of chin.

Greater-thans:
unopened ears.

Four paws cleaved
to clawed digits.

Blade of pink grass.
Small lungs,

lucky thumbs
swelled by one

hammer's blow
of breath.

## To M, on Memory

In my only photo of you, taken
near the oasis at Al-Bahariya,
you grin with the other men
around the squat dinner table,
bright batik windbreak shielding you
from the questions night
asks the desert.

The darkened curve of dune and pallid sand
gleam like the road
to heaven—other beauties
to fill the gaps of you. I'm in love

with image, but since I know
the road that shimmers
leads to hell, it's this I'll keep:
your unexpected touch before dawn
as you leaned to tuck my slipped blanket
around me, then went back to sleep.

## What the Angel Gabriel Said

The difference now lies only in our bodies:
your little grain of sand robing itself
in layers of pearl, but more:
knowledge crystallizing
from some forgotten pocket
in each cell until you are *mother.*

I think *if it were me,* and all that loveliness
dims and sinks as beneath water.
Selfishness, always the lowest
common denominator.
I praise my freedom:
time to sleep, leave to drink,
travel, ample passion,
slow motion.
Simple things that could fill a life.

Your mandala,
paperwhite blossoms, stars—
so much beauty born from the dark.
Who can tell when it will come,
the abrupt catapult to *chosen*?
Your gift is not just happiness
but in knowing the finite
ways we possess to love,
in learning them all.

## Hard Days

Oracles babble: *it's coming,*
*be ready.* Deliveries from Fate
can't be picked up later,
may explode while waiting

on your doorstep.
The days spool out their
varicolored terrors. We try
to escape, but everything

beyond arm's reach
grows waxy with fog.
Instead, we sit, glowering children,
our mistakes served up to us

like the dinner we must finish
before leaving the table,
Mother fussing
in a dead language.

# ii HOW WE LEARNED TO LET GO

## Lord's Prayer

My father taught it the old-fashioned way,
alien and ornate as a wafer on the tongue.

*Thine* for *your, art* for *are*—
new words for words I knew

at three years old.
I don't remember

what I meant when I asked God
to deliver me, to forgive things

I didn't know I'd someday do.
*Trespass,* Dad explained, was sin:

going where you didn't belong,
off the narrow path of goodness

into the glittery forest.
He made no mention

of the sin not
mortal or venial

but liminal, embedded
in you the way life is,

a simple thing decanted
deep inside the bone.

He was as smart as God,
my father. He drove off

and never returned, the words
that would absolve him

set pealing long ago,
helpless bells to open heaven.

# Double Birth

*for my sister*

Suddenly the hours gaped
into a hole we
all fell through,

the fearful moment
when you were nothing,
an absence, and all there was

was a wheel slowly turning.
Your mother's skin yawned,
a vase of negative space

spilling petals of dark blood.
And then your head, the pallid
muck that coated your limbs,

torso, fingers. I saw them move
like replicas, like machines.
Your skin pinked. Then you cried

as I did, astonished,
indignant,
brought against your will

into a room of believers
gathered to drown you
in love, in air.

## Notes on Summer

i.
The day after we arrived
Dad left for work.
You slid off the cold leather couches.
I braided the rug's white fringe.

When he returned, he set
his briefcase on the smudged glass table
and went outside. We stared into the black gut
of the barbecue grill. I held you back
as he stacked briquets, showed us how to leave
a secret space in the center where the haze
of lighter fluid would curl, wait to burst.

ii.
I dressed you for story hour, white ribbon
in your red-gold hair.
Your palms
engraved with dirt.
Blue jumper
with yellow duck—
I fumed
at your small face.

iii.
In the backyard Dad lit cherry bombs.
Their blue bodies whirled, spit
smoke, died in flame.
The girlfriend I loved, dark-
curled Maylene,
stayed with me behind
the porch door glass,
stroked my head resting
on her bare leg.

iv.
You laughed
as I soaked the packs of Marlboros.
He tried to light
a sodden smoke,
swore and chucked them
at the wall, then clipped
a saved cigar.
On the hallway stairs, I cried.
After that we hid cancer warnings
in his bathrobe pockets—
black-markered lungs, leaflet death tolls—
or taped them to the door.

v.
To welcome us, he'd bought
outlandish lamps shaped like candles,
draped narrow new beds
in cotton comforters,
yours peach, mine sea-green.
A cluster of colored balloons
butted the ceiling, trailing ribbons like smoke.
Nights, I stared at
that electric lavender waver
burning close and false.
You oohed at those balloons.
I warned you they would fall eventually.

vi.
The sky on the way back to Wisconsin faltered.
He zagged the car
through rain that snapped
off the windshield, filled
the floorboards of the Plymouth.
I watched my library book
float, nudge my ankles.
You slept in the back seat,
open-mouthed—
fog rose from ditches.

## How We Learned to Let Go

Water lilted around my ankles,
my library book caroming
like a waiter's tray.
The floorboards soaked through,
the faded mats the color now
of cool loam, as Dad sped
the Valiant northward into the rain.
Brittle plastic peeled
from the book's paper cover,
the picture of a forest, a cottage
winking within.
I knew once I got home
Mom would lift the sopping book
without saying *it,*
the same thing
I wanted to say to him:
*Look what you did.*
But after he drove away,
after she'd asked like a stranger
about his job, the name of his girlfriend—
we'd both think it,
as the book grew light
on the heating vent,
rain rattling up from the pages
and down onto the street.

## Her Hair

I used to say I envied her
ease, her happy-go-lucky *whatever.*
But it was her hair,
sun in filaments,
that I stared at.

Our father was dark. He moved
like a traveling salesman, snapping
his case open and shut with burning
eagerness, farther and farther from home.

I was dark. I rode the bus
to buy goldfish at the mall.
At night I walked down to the lake,
touched its silver tongue
out for the moon's communion.

She was born with that shining,
seeming proof of difference,
what he called *spun gold*
as he brushed it with the baby brush
and tied it into pigtails—
my missing buoyancy,
his secret, happy
self.

# A Family of Expatriates from the Territories of Crazy

It was a one-liner
to me, a soft shoe
of shock. Easier to tell
with a smile: my uncle and his crow
calls, my mythical grandmother.
Others were luckier,
airlifted on lithium.

When I started shopping nonstop,
smoking till the coffeeshop closed
after I cheated on my first boyfriend,
I went to a shrink, ready to collect
what I'd come to think of
as my inheritance.

"Sounds like you don't love him,"
he barked. "Break up with him."
I was sick with lust and credit card debt.
I walked home plugged into my earphones.

I'd been holding out my hands
for what was coming,
squinting so hard into the sky
I didn't even recognize it

when it fell, swift
as a cartoon anvil,
and crushed her.

## Late Arrival

I imagined him pulling up to the curb
in a steel-gray rental car. He'd plant his feet
on the asphalt and close the door.

I saw him silhouetted from behind,
as a man in a movie would be,
pausing in front of the house

in evening's transparent light,
with leaves ricocheting across the grass.
I wanted a hero's stride,

a forthright gesture ending
wordlessly, tearfully
as he held her crumpling body.

Then she would know all this
was just a movement toward memory,
one of many hard times we'd forget.

## October

I made her childhood's foods,
macaroni and cheese, green beans,
applesauce. I ate.
Nothing could stay in her.
Her body would drive her out.

We looked at her senior pictures,
taken some time ago. Recognition had drained
from her face even then.
Her hands had formed angles around
her face, odd juxtapositions of bone
and softness. Her clothes tried

to make her older: a silver lavalier,
an off-the-shoulder blouse
struggling against her puzzled expression.

Those nights, I turned in my hotel bed,
as she lay stagnant-eyed
in a room that sometimes dripped
with the sound of her drowning.

But at most times
she was still, a beach
clean of sand,
a thick blank sky.

## Beachgrass

The backyard sand loomed ineluctably
lunar: nightscape transformed
into a glowing undulation of white.
The lake licked the edge of the universe.
Past the beachgrass were answers
or questions. I didn't know.
I paid attention only to sorrow,
which I tried (as I did
with everything) to take in my arms.
But it grew as I held it,
flowed from me, overtaking
the floor I stood on, the house,
my field of vision.
It was good preparation,
though not enough.

## A Bridge-Building Competition

was our theme one day in sixth-grade science.
We each received materials: cardboard,
string, short plastic straws. Tape and glue.
I stared at them like I stared at Indian food.
I thought of large cities, rivers spanned
by swoops of steel against the sky.
I made that, a plank of cardboard
with a cage of straws rising crooked off its top.

In one of my houses, no one had my name
but me. When I was with my dad and sister,
we shared it. All poems
are elegies. To list
the things I remember about her
would be to act like she's dead,
but that would be mistaking her for me.

The weight the teacher loaded on
collapsed my bridge easily.
The bridge that won was made
entirely of cardboard, folded
around and around itself
in a triangle. Just a triangle.
*The strongest shape,* the teacher nodded.

## Duty

i.
I will never forget the phone call:
the tears shaking from me,
the enormous bed I lay on
as I tried to pull you from the edge with my voice.
What you told me—somehow,
it never surprised me.
You couldn't say no to guys, would do whatever they wanted—
the rest didn't make sense, and that
was the most frightening part.
No food could reach you, no rest.
You were so tired.

Clearly there is wrong, blame
moving like a cloud of angry bees, never settling.
It wounds each of us in turn.

Our father didn't come. You seemed about to die
in a house full of strangers.
I got in the car, I came for you.

ii.
Their family room was filled with Rena's workspace,
her odd assortment of materials for sculpture—
pine cones, ribbons, paints—
and everything else was upstairs.
It was so strange to find that you had a room
in their house.

Things identified it as yours: pictures of people I knew
including myself, papers with your name on them.
A poster of a rapper,
a surfing collage—expressions of desires
I didn't know you had. The colors of the room
were aquamarine and green. False brightness.

iii.

It was not like I knew what to do.
I took you to the doctor,
got a prescription that we filled,
then urged you to take the medicine.
I don't remember if you went to school,
perhaps it was the weekend.
The way your face looked is what I remember,
the distance between where you were and me.
I was glad when you cried
because it brought you back, gave you a shape.

I took you and Sophia to the video store, terrified
to pick out the wrong movie.
Rena made us little pizzas. You ate some and threw it up later.

iv.

I came once more
to take you to my home.
I am afraid to be irrelevant in the world.
I cried in secret. Your tears
were public,
you merely seemed
to witness them as one would
the coming of the mail.

In a few days I took you back to Sophia's family.
I am still ashamed of it.

v.

The medicine was doing funny things to you.
I didn't trust your doctor.
Suddenly your sleeping parents began to mobilize
from their corners of the country,

Dad shaking off the sunshine, your mom taking the back roads
into the airport city. I went to Durham to help you
put things in boxes, do whatever you could not.
Dad was due in at eleven that night, so I left at eight.
I could not look in his face, I would not
have said I loved him.

vi.
When I visited him months later,
he asked me if I blamed him.

You were the car we got in,
the twisted road we drove into the mountains,
the ground we buried each other in,
the grass that grows over our graves.
What use have I been
to either of you?

## Elegy for My Father's Third Family

The cab pulls up to the blank apartment.
It could be Illinois, Indiana, Carolina:
the blue-rimmed dishes,
scattered scraps of paper bearing your scrawl.
This time you offer me beer, let me sleep in.

The highway from Santa Cruz
sashays along the ocean,
pink spray of bougainvillea tucked
behind its ear. You mutter
about this last wife: rich as cream,
wrecked by indelicate handling.
Out there, one more stranger
who used to be family.

In North Beach you order the wine sampler,
white-pleated waiter filling your glass
with the dribbled moonlight of Chardonnay.
He brings elegant pizza and, for you,
the reds. Calf's-blood Merlot, doe-eyed Shiraz.
In the belly of the glass dregs mingle,
luck and inevitability.

At the gate we bring out our tattered good-byes.
The ground falls away like a veil.
I rise on a widening wedge of air
over the bright machine of your new city:
dirty sidewalks and watch shops,
blue banner of water that you cross in awe.

## Place of Last Escape

He took me there once
on a business trip when I was twelve, just us.
While he went to meetings
I sat in a bookstore ecstatic,

and when he was not occupied
we ate butterfly cookies in Chinatown.
The drive up the Pacific Coast highway,
my first tiramisu, my first plane ride—

all these I gave up
to a poem. In the page's
dark distance, they float:
lit, discrete

under their singular spotlights.
Now, what it meant
to buy fifty-cent sandalwood soaps
or peek behind the bars at Alcatraz

is, itself,
a memory.

## Interlude

I saw my life
as though from a plane:
not the mottled greens

of thirty thousand feet,
but the way a town looks
as the descent begins:

the buildings curiosities,
the fly-sized people
ruthlessly laughable.

And when I returned,
all that was small
had burst to spacious,

whole rooms and cars
to hold me, and I
loved it that much more.

## My Father's Fruit Trees

My imagination rolled lustily
over them on the plane to California.
The reckless romance

of tender flesh collared
in leaf, married to branch.
To contain such waywardness

in your own backyard
perplexed a midwestern sensibility.
But his birthplace was just

a sliding screen door
that he walked through
on his way to this lushness,

a bounty for his collecting.
Orange trees, Valencia and navel,
lemons, limes, and a peach—

I walked out to greet them
as though to long-lost sisters.
Their green skins bloomed

with gray—pitilessly
hard, anonymous.
I picked them with some cruelty.

And one morning
he squeezed them, still green,
grunting, forcing resistant

bodies onto the juicer's spike,
spilling pale fluid and seeds.
We drank silently then, waiting

to see who would admit first
the sting of unripe lemon,
not orange, burning in our throats.

## Acquittal

I saw it in a movie once, the grace
I wanted for you:

an old woman who had done so much wrong
she hunkered under it like a beast

was suddenly embraced by a young girl
she'd just met. You could see it

on her face as the girl fell
into her arms: she had stopped believing

there was anyone in the world
who didn't know her mistakes.

Not love, but lack
of accusation. A fresh wind.

I wanted to be that girl, who couldn't see
anything but a sorrowful old lady

in the woman who'd abandoned
children and husband

in the only choice she'd ever made.
I see sometimes through you,

into the dream of a real marriage,
the envy you burn so low

one might think it had gone out.
To every flu you've nursed yourself through,

the unspeakable amount of my life
you missed. Then I give it over

to some stranger I hope will find you,
the burden of forgiving you.

## The Tourist

Not ten minutes after
we've hung up, the phone rings
again: *I need advice,* he says.

A flush of pleasure. Then:
*I have this camera.*
Coded buttons,
mysterious symbols.

I tell him: the flower
means drawing close;
the arrow, the direction
of one's intentions;
the face, triumph
of light over shadow.

What happened to the manual?
*I'm in Golden Gate Park,* he says—
not two miles from his house—

and my love rushes fumbling,
silent, into his lonely Sunday.

# iii LETTERS FROM THE ELISION

## Letters from the Elision

*Dearest S,*

I woke last night with a ribbon of sweat at my throat. There's no other way to say this—you'll think it's uncharacteristically bold of me, but how much you don't know!—I dreamed your taste in my mouth, like a starred silence after beating wings.

*My incandescent S,*

Find my hook-and-eye: I've come unlatched. Clasp me, as in the old romances. You can offer me your handkerchief and my virtue. I'll dampen you with tears and tuck you inside my camisole.

*My quiet S,*

My god in the garden, my violets and roses. The dip and swoop of landscape, your back and percussive thigh.

*S, my distant S,*

Night air strokes the morning glories, coaxes their prim buds. I lie awake and ignore the dreams, listen to the pilot light murmur its blue language.

*My sleeping, dreaming S,*

I'm a sailor's lost button, the anchor of your shoulders carved into my heart's black celluloid. Next time I won't use your initial, I swear it. I am still the same sweet one amidst the coloratura of my confessions. I'll leave the porch door open, until night comes—

## The Chapter of Faults

### NOVICE: A FRONTISPIECE

A living thing is entering
the window. Watch the dark
walls scabbed with light.

Hunger has filigreed
her face like a flower,
supple relief of dusky veins.
She rocks warily, baring
her tapestry of bruise
and hair, the glyph of bone
like a locket holding a secret.

When he called her into
the scent of animal wetness—
a wink of dank crevice.
When he crept down
the black nave of breath.

A gift of brocade, a specimen of lavender.
Take as much with you
as you can grasp in your hand: acorn,
slipper, eyebright.

Frame him a last time: his nativity
smelled of chemicals, his vespers too.

### THE OPENING DOOR

As the first fingers of light coax the dew,
larks sing in the cage of vines
that lines the convent wall.

Hesper turns in her muslin pocket.
The photography chemicals have eaten her hands,
their skin hardened and shredded.
Pewter, skin, the picture
she took of him, his face

hidden in gray grain.
She waits to hear his steps:

*my Hesper, my help,*
*my hyacinth, my hierophant,*

*my halo.*

## ABSENCE

Her skin glazes and beads,
the firing and misfiring
leaving her surface stretched,
pocked with hazard.

The linen square withers
on her forehead.
Outside, trees scratch their names on the wind
but no one can read them.
The sisters wait for her to come back,
their palms upturned.

## THE CHAPTER OF FAULTS

Mother Superior studies silkscreening
and the life cycle of bats.
My study is the Great Silence,
silverish text of emptiness.

*Mea culpa, mea culpa.*
I accuse myself to you, dear Mother.
In my hand the Discipline
writhes, nine wires dancing.

Among the voided evidence:
paper-pale hand, bile-dark bird,
a scream of flowers gathered
in a slender glass throat.

§

## THE BIRTH

When he looked at her palms
she grew ashamed
because he was thinking of Jesus's wounds.

*We are not like Him,* she said
the last time they saw each other.
The shards of skin snagged
wool and muslin, making it difficult
to touch anything.

§

The luscious weight of the Cross
startles her acid-knitted hand.
She looks over at the wooden table,
the sweating kettle.
Pain like a brilliant dawn
on the first day of anything.
This is God, the angry clarity
unmistakable.
*He has been inside me all along,* she thinks,
and her flesh splits according to her doubt.

*Dearest S,*

Autumn. The landscape glows with sacrifice. Black fences pickstitched on yellow hills. All the dying, the glorious giving over. *Fallow* I know. *Done with* I know. Spent clouds, red-brown cattle searching for a green thing to muzzle.

*Traipse:* after you like the train on a bridal gown. *Float:* low over cobblestones where feet go.

I search the places you like to hide—

in a dell, in a dale, in the dropping sequins of the leaves.

## *My S—*

Would you send a letter with words scratched out? What the black crosshatchings conceal seems so personal, so private. But if I am shepherd of rejected words, I'll unpen them to graze and grow. Then you'll get *clamor.* Then you'll get *so.*

## Anthem

She studies herself. Like bread dough,
roped swells merge.

Mountains wimpled in remainder-light.
The dark tappings of birds on the sky.

She studies herself. Covered
with a cloth like bread dough.

Mountains upjutting. A long low
comfort of grass. Lying there
like recognition. A starting point,
a colophon.

§

Her legs like rough trees—hewed, they
would make a sturdy ship. She remembers
rocking in the water, flannel and woodlight
                                                                                O her rocking.

And her legs cut water to breath-bright streamers.
Propelling was her main joy.
In water she slid, both sail and fish.
Her steep sides hold the silver bounty still—
                                                                                a myriad of fish.

The nice trimmings,
                    a lace of white sugar
and a collar of cream,
                                        are in her elsewhere.

Her backbone of cockled pearl, loyal knots between.
Her ass a soft forgetting.

A pleasure. Fuzzed as fruit.
A carnation shirred and gathered.

She is whole
when she remembers it.

§

In her arms she rests most-at-home.
The double crescents of her muscles wax.

Were she a boat she would row her across the world.
O, and sleep soundly, O and sleep well,
riches in her sleeping smile.

It is the grabbing and not-getting that makes these arms strong.

She lifts herself up and sees,
over the other side of the mountains,
the river limned with light.

§

Legs tread the mountains' spine.
Arms sag the sky's weight.

Lightning genuflects:
lumined black. Over
the mountains: her own image.

She squeezes her eyes shut to lock up a sigh.
She hears it struggle.
She will carry it in her teeth.

*My dear S,*

It's getting to be too much, sleep just this crucible. In the morning I awaken formless and white-hot with dreams. A fireball blooming like a peony in a crowded street. A ruined building—I soared through it, workers stilling their implements and raising their heads to stare.

And then your face—your face—

I wake full of disconnections, intensities that take up residence behind my ribs. Day sublimates them, but when I lie down to sleep they rattle and howl again, as if time tied itself in a bow, and the dream just ended.

—your face, dying, crazed like a pane of glass. O, but your eyes—your eyes were as clear as Tuesday.

## Letter Home

Have I told you how easy it is to sleep now, while what is supple bleeds out of the day, the sky going flat and burnished? I sleep until my bones soften with sleep, until my tongue swells with sleep, until my lips are stitched by sleep.

Days, the sun raises blisters of fuchsia on the crape myrtles. I stare through an intaglio of mountain inked blue on the sky's pale paper. Do you hear that old self coming down the peeling steps of the house? Small reflection in a spoon, upside down. She is hemming my life to her, heel and wrist, like Peter Pan's shadow—a family putting their arms around each other, neat as a row of teeth. A dog and a green world of yard for him to run in.

A ladder leans against the house, just outside my window. When I dream, I see myself rising: a hand gripping the rung, blowing hair, two ciphered eyes. I rouse myself like a dull child when moonlight remainders up from the gutters and nightbirds fly their flags of ragged sound. Down in the groundwater, useless things unfurl their toxic secrets.

*My drifting S,*

I hear your hot voice slinking among wet leaves, large-eyed animals slowing their limbs to listen. I can't reach—you've got to come to me,

come to me—

In your absence I recited a poem. An intricate pink rhyme I sewed around your name. I have all frills for you. I would tuck you in a big bed and brush your hair as you slept.

I stitch silk on a square of homespun. A peacock on the lawn.

*Dear S,*

The grass is seething like petted fur. The bronze pollen infects my hair, makes me invincible. I picture what I imagine as your city: its shapely metallic expression a harshness on the earth. Will you pump like a heart while it shakes its steel into piles? Little warmth in my cupped hand. Little needle.

*My ache, my S—*

Climb the steps to my kitchen and together we'll open the notebooks. I'll watch as you relight your candle, settle your foolscap, and fall asleep with your cheek pressed to the table. Your face at rest makes me smile in the dark.

Until I hear from you—and I expect to, I will be watching the sky's twilit kimono—

*Fervently,*

# iv THE HOUSE OF MARRIAGE

## The Difficulty of Compline on a Train

I have grasped a bit
of the evening to say my prayer,
before I angle my head against
    the hard plate of glass
to sleep.

The locomotive planes us down into night,
        quietness spilling like fuel.

The moon floats, a pearl onion,
but

                    God is delicately somewhere

in that heaven, with its branches,
brushstrokes of japan, enduring and glossy,

trees and train skimming
the surface of the sky.

## For an Unnamed Brother

He was a half-moon above
Mother's elbow: the head, the dove-

white ears—delicate conchs
mottled blue under a monk's

fringe of shimmering hair.
Each small part of him was silent, smeared

with trying.
His dying

coated the insides of our skulls,
dripped continuously, dulled

the world's sharpness like a drug.
Living, tugged

by death,
we left

the trees unraveling black moss
under a moon as voluptuous and dazzling as loss.

## The House of Marriage

*for CZ*

It's the scariest house on the block,
to be sure. I've been warned
but I go like mischief,
wandering hallways, opening doors.
The stillness is enormous;
no one's lived within these walls
who survived, at least
none I know of. But artifacts prove
some have tried. I've lived
through pictures of their wedding:
her slim body humming
like a mandolin under lace,
her intact smile.
And him—enigmatic child
in his confident gray suit.
Here, their scents
layer in the air—
her White Linen, his cigarette smoke,
settled in wallpaper curled by tears' heat,
sunk in carpet discolored by grief.
No other proof or clue remains,
no photographs, no bed.
This place is as fearful
as they said.
I want to see them
move through it like water,
luscious and damaging,
toward the moment
that made me. I want
to watch them suffer.
I want to know
that they are no mirror.
Come live with me
and be my love. We'll build
our house from ground.

## Conception

After making you,

then

I knew I would die.
The way

the sun lifted green
from the leaves

on the trees along the highway

was how I'd go:
implacable, serene
veined transparency.

The after-image of a being

penetrated by light.